THE FAMILY Chronicle OF

Written and created by Judy Lawrence

Published by

Lawrence & Co. Publishers
P.O. Box 13167
Albuquerque, NM 87192

Copyright 1987 by Lawrence & Co. Publishers.
All rights reserved.
Printed in the United States of America.
No part of this publication may be reproduced,
stored in a retrieval system, or transmitted,
in any form or by any means, electronic, mechanical,
photocopying, recording, or otherwise,
without the prior written permission of the publisher.

Book design by Sherri Holtke.
Front cover design by Ken Wilson.

ISBN 0-9607096-5-7

This book may be ordered directly from the publisher.
Try your bookstore or giftstore first.

INTRODUCTION

Dear Friend:

Do the years and events seem to pass by so quickly that they suddenly just become hazy memories? *The Family Chronicle* is designed to keep your memories intact by being a complementary companion to photo albums, home movies, baby books, school scrapbooks, grandparent books and other keepsakes.

❖

Keeping in mind your busy lifestyle, *The Family Chronicle* is simple and efficient to use so you can organize and capture favorite memories forever. The format allows you to jot down a summary of what you did on any holiday or special occasion — just enough to jog your memory later on when you reminisce about life's special moments. If you received a special gift, gave an exceptional party, celebrated a 25th wedding anniversary, remodeled your kitchen, enjoyed a memorable reunion or got together with old friends not seen in years, here is the place to record it all.

❖

When you have completed the five-year record in *The Family Chronicle* you will have a storehouse of memories and information in a convenient and easily-accessible book. *You will have captured the essence of the last five years* instead of feeling as if the years just passed by in a blur.

❖

I hope you enjoy using this memory book as much as I enjoyed creating it.

Judy Lawrence
Judy Lawrence

CONTENTS

HOW TO START	6
RECORDING HOLIDAYS & EVENTS	7
CHRISTMAS	9
NEW YEAR'S	22
EASTER	24
MEMORIAL DAY	26
4TH OF JULY	28
LABOR DAY	30
THANKSGIVING	33
SPECIAL CELEBRATIONS	37
BIRTHDAYS	45
WEDDING ANNIVERSARIES	53
CHILDREN'S MILESTONES	57
TRIPS & VACATIONS	65
GUESTS & VISITORS	69
PARTIES HOSTED	73
ADDITIONAL EVENTS & RECORDS	81
MISCELLANEOUS	93

◆

HOW TO START

This is your book — use it the best way that suits your style for summarizing yearly highlights.

◆

Decide what year you want to begin your records. It could be this year, your wedding year, or the year of a turning point in your life.

◆

By no means should your notes be limited to summaries only. If you enjoy recording all the wonderful details on any particular event, an Additional Remarks page is provided at the back of each section.

◆

On the other hand, some holidays may be no different than the average day. Rather than leave that section blank, jot down a comment (e.g. "nothing special — worked all day") just as a reminder for distinguishing the events of one year from another.

◆

The Family Chronicle allows you to record your memories in the way that best suits your lifestyle. If you find that a particular event is more appropriate on a page different than suggested, record the event on the page that best fits your needs.

◆

RECORDING HOLIDAYS & EVENTS

Do you remember how you spent New Year's Eve or the 4th of July five years ago? What about birthdays or vacations? *The Family Chronicle* provides record pages for describing many aspects of the special occasions in your life.

◆

In this book, you will find places to remember the major holidays, including Christmas, New Year's, Easter, Memorial Day, 4th of July, Labor Day, and Thanksgiving. In these sections you can note those Easter egg hunts, parades, fireworks, parties, or people which were a part of the holiday celebration.

◆

In addition, space is provided, in the Special Celebrations Section, for other holidays that are celebrated by your family. On these pages, you can keep track of events such as Hanukkah, Passover, Valentine's Day, St. Patrick's Day, or Veteran's Day.

◆

Finally, *The Family Chronicle* includes pages for noting Birthdays, Anniversaries, Children's Milestones, Trips and Vacations, Guests and Visitors, Parties Hosted, and Additional Events and Records. These pages are ideal for summarizing and highlighting various activities and accomplishments of your family.

◆

The Family Chronicle is designed to help you get started, but it is your own special memories that make this book a cherished treasure.

◆

CHRISTMAS

Christmas season is the highlight of the year for many families. You can easily fill up several pages with your Christmas memories of religious observations, presents under the tree, gathering of family and friends, parties, toasts, traditional meals, and special treats.

◆

Many families have different activities occurring on Christmas Eve and Christmas Day, as well as the whole week, so you may want to record a great deal of information. Decide what you especially want to remember and describe it on the following yearly pages.

◆

If there is more information than space available be selective and note only the very special gifts and moments or use extra space on the Additional Remarks page.

◆

In addition to preserving cherished memories, the gift information you record can help prevent duplicate gift giving in the future.

◆

CHRISTMAS

19____

LOCATION	OTHERS PRESENT	ACTIVITIES

GIFTS GIVEN

Given To: Gift Item:

CHRISTMAS

TRADITIONS OBSERVED	WEATHER	SPECIAL MEALS & RECIPES ENJOYED

GIFTS RECEIVED

Received From:	Gift Item:

CHRISTMAS

19____

LOCATION	OTHERS PRESENT	ACTIVITIES

GIFTS GIVEN

Given To: Gift Item:

CHRISTMAS

TRADITIONS OBSERVED	WEATHER	SPECIAL MEALS & RECIPES ENJOYED
_____	_____	_____
_____	_____	_____
_____	_____	_____
_____	_____	_____
_____	_____	_____
_____	_____	_____
_____	_____	_____
_____	_____	_____

GIFTS RECEIVED

Received From:	Gift Item:
_____	_____
_____	_____
_____	_____
_____	_____
_____	_____
_____	_____
_____	_____
_____	_____
_____	_____
_____	_____
_____	_____

CHRISTMAS

19____

LOCATION   OTHERS PRESENT   ACTIVITIES

GIFTS GIVEN

Given To: Gift Item:

CHRISTMAS

TRADITIONS OBSERVED	WEATHER	SPECIAL MEALS & RECIPES ENJOYED
_____	_____	_____
_____	_____	_____
_____	_____	_____
_____	_____	_____
_____	_____	_____
_____	_____	_____
_____	_____	_____
_____	_____	_____

GIFTS RECEIVED

Received From:	Gift Item:
_____	_____
_____	_____
_____	_____
_____	_____
_____	_____
_____	_____
_____	_____
_____	_____
_____	_____
_____	_____
_____	_____
_____	_____

CHRISTMAS

19_____

LOCATION   OTHERS PRESENT   ACTIVITIES

GIFTS GIVEN

Given To: Gift Item:

CHRISTMAS

TRADITIONS OBSERVED	WEATHER	SPECIAL MEALS & RECIPES ENJOYED

GIFTS RECEIVED

Received From: Gift Item:

CHRISTMAS

19____

LOCATION OTHERS PRESENT ACTIVITIES

GIFTS GIVEN

Given To: Gift Item:

CHRISTMAS

TRADITIONS OBSERVED	WEATHER	SPECIAL MEALS & RECIPES ENJOYED
_____	_____	_____
_____	_____	_____
_____	_____	_____
_____	_____	_____
_____	_____	_____
_____	_____	_____
_____	_____	_____
_____	_____	_____

GIFTS RECEIVED

Received From:	Gift Item:
_____	_____
_____	_____
_____	_____
_____	_____
_____	_____
_____	_____
_____	_____
_____	_____
_____	_____
_____	_____
_____	_____
_____	_____

ADDITIONAL REMARKS

YEAR COMMENTS

19____

19____

19____

19____

19____

ADDITIONAL REMARKS

COMMENTS

NEW YEAR'S
Eve/Day

19____

Location: _____

Others With: _____

Activities: _____

Traditions Observed: _____

19____

Location: _____

Others With: _____

Activities: _____

Traditions Observed: _____

19____

Location: _____

Others With: _____

Activities: _____

Traditions Observed: _____

19____

Location: _____

Others With: _____

Activities: _____

Traditions Observed: _____

19____

Location: _____

Others With: _____

Activities: _____

Traditions Observed: _____

ADDITIONAL REMARKS

YEAR   COMMENTS

19____

19____

19____

19____

19____

EASTER

19____

Location: _____ Activities: _____
_____ _____
_____ _____

Others With: _____ Traditions Observed: _____
_____ _____
_____ _____

19____

Location: _____ Activities: _____
_____ _____
_____ _____

Others With: _____ Traditions Observed: _____
_____ _____
_____ _____

19____

Location: _____ Activities: _____
_____ _____
_____ _____

Others With: _____ Traditions Observed: _____
_____ _____
_____ _____

19____

Location: _____ Activities: _____
_____ _____
_____ _____

Others With: _____ Traditions Observed: _____
_____ _____
_____ _____

19____

Location: _____ Activities: _____
_____ _____
_____ _____

Others With: _____ Traditions Observed: _____
_____ _____
_____ _____

ADDITIONAL REMARKS

YEAR   COMMENTS

19____

19____

19____

19____

19____

MEMORIAL DAY

19____

Location: _____   Activities: _____
_____   _____
_____   _____
_____   _____

Others With: _____   Traditions Observed: _____
_____   _____
_____   _____
_____   _____

19____

Location: _____   Activities: _____
_____   _____
_____   _____
_____   _____

Others With: _____   Traditions Observed: _____
_____   _____
_____   _____
_____   _____

19____

Location: _____   Activities: _____
_____   _____
_____   _____
_____   _____

Others With: _____   Traditions Observed: _____
_____   _____
_____   _____
_____   _____

19____

Location: _____   Activities: _____
_____   _____
_____   _____
_____   _____

Others With: _____   Traditions Observed: _____
_____   _____
_____   _____
_____   _____

19____

Location: _____   Activities: _____
_____   _____
_____   _____
_____   _____

Others With: _____   Traditions Observed: _____
_____   _____
_____   _____
_____   _____

ADDITIONAL REMARKS

YEAR   COMMENTS

19____   _____
          _____
          _____
          _____
          _____
          _____
          _____

19____   _____
          _____
          _____
          _____
          _____
          _____
          _____

19____   _____
          _____
          _____
          _____
          _____
          _____
          _____

19____   _____
          _____
          _____
          _____
          _____
          _____
          _____

19____   _____
          _____
          _____
          _____
          _____
          _____
          _____

4th of JULY

19____

Location: _____

Activities: _____

Others With: _____

Traditions Observed: _____

19____

Location: _____

Activities: _____

Others With: _____

Traditions Observed: _____

19____

Location: _____

Activities: _____

Others With: _____

Traditions Observed: _____

19____

Location: _____

Activities: _____

Others With: _____

Traditions Observed: _____

19____

Location: _____

Activities: _____

Others With: _____

Traditions Observed: _____

ADDITIONAL REMARKS

YEAR COMMENTS

19____

19____

19____

19____

19____

LABOR DAY

19____

Location: _____

Activities: _____

Others With: _____

Traditions Observed: _____

19____

Location: _____

Activities: _____

Others With: _____

Traditions Observed: _____

19____

Location: _____

Activities: _____

Others With: _____

Traditions Observed: _____

19____

Location: _____

Activities: _____

Others With: _____

Traditions Observed: _____

19____

Location: _____

Activities: _____

Others With: _____

Traditions Observed: _____

ADDITIONAL REMARKS

YEAR COMMENTS

19____

19____

19____

19____

19____

THANKSGIVING

Thanksgiving marks the beginning of the holiday season and the gathering of relatives and friends for the traditional turkey dinner. Whether you continue to follow this tradition or have your own way of celebrating, Thanksgiving is always a holiday to remember.

◆

Perhaps it is the baby's first Thanksgiving, or the first time in a long time all the adult children are home together. What special meals and wine did you enjoy? Is there a toast you want to remember? Did you go somewhere or do something worth noting?

◆

Use the following pages for recording the *highlights* of your Thanksgiving celebration.

◆

THANKSGIVING

DATES	LOCATION	OTHERS PRESENT	ACTIVITIES
19____	_____	_____	_____
19____	_____	_____	_____
19____	_____	_____	_____
19____	_____	_____	_____
19____	_____	_____	_____

THANKSGIVING

TRADITIONS OBSERVED

SPECIAL MEALS
& RECIPES ENJOYED

ADDITIONAL REMARKS

YEAR　　　　　　　　　　COMMENTS

19____

19____

19____

19____

19____

SPECIAL CELEBRATIONS

Every family celebrates many different holidays and events. Since there is not enough room to include all holidays individually, this section is provided so you can record the special days and occasions unique to you that you want to remember.

◆

Perhaps a ski trip on Presidents' Day weekend, a nice gift on Secretary's or Boss's Day are special one year. Another year may bring a unique Valentine's Day present, a St. Patrick's Day party or your favorite team in the Superbowl or World Series.

◆

Special Celebrations can also include events such as Bar Mitzvahs, Confirmations, Baptisms, graduations, Father's and Mother's Day or a Golden Anniversary. Don't forget your annual canoe trip, wine-tasting party or open house celebration for your new home.

◆

Decide which holidays and happenings you want to remember, and include them on the following yearly pages. This is a good place to include all those miscellaneous events and activities you don't want to forget.

◆

SPECIAL CELEBRATIONS

19____

DATE	SPECIAL CELEBRATION EVENTS

SPECIAL CELEBRATIONS

19_____

DATE   SPECIAL CELEBRATION EVENTS

SPECIAL CELEBRATIONS

19____

DATE   SPECIAL CELEBRATION EVENTS

SPECIAL CELEBRATIONS

19____

DATE　　　　　　　　　SPECIAL CELEBRATION EVENTS

SPECIAL CELEBRATIONS

19____

DATE   SPECIAL CELEBRATION EVENTS

ADDITIONAL REMARKS

YEAR COMMENTS

19____

19____

19____

19____

19____

BIRTHDAYS

For children — and for many adults — birthdays are very important.

◆

On the following pages you will find room for recording those days of special recognition for all members of your family. What presents were received? From whom? Was there a party or other observance to mark the day?

◆

If you keep a short record for each year you will be able to look back and see which type of birthday celebrations you want to repeat. You can also see which gifts were received and avoid giving a duplicate gift later.

If you need more room for recording the birthday celebrations of people outside your immediate family — aunts, uncles, grandparents and cousins — use the Additional Remarks page at the end of this section.

◆

Have a Happy Birthday!

◆

BIRTHDAYS

19_____

NAME	AGE	HOW CELEBRATED (location, activities, others present)	GIFTS

BIRTHDAYS

19____

NAME	AGE	HOW CELEBRATED (location, activities, others present)	GIFTS

BIRTHDAYS

19____

NAME	AGE	HOW CELEBRATED *(location, activities, others present)*	GIFTS
_____	___	_____	_____
		_____	_____
		_____	_____
_____	___	_____	_____
		_____	_____
		_____	_____
_____	___	_____	_____
		_____	_____
		_____	_____
_____	___	_____	_____
		_____	_____
		_____	_____
_____	___	_____	_____
		_____	_____
		_____	_____
_____	___	_____	_____
		_____	_____
		_____	_____
_____	___	_____	_____
		_____	_____
		_____	_____
_____	___	_____	_____
		_____	_____
		_____	_____

BIRTHDAYS

19_____

NAME	AGE	HOW CELEBRATED *(location, activities, others present)*	GIFTS

BIRTHDAYS

19_____

NAME	AGE	HOW CELEBRATED *(location, activities, others present)*	GIFTS

ADDITIONAL REMARKS

YEAR　　　　　　　　　　　COMMENTS

19____

19____

19____

19____

19____

WEDDING ANNIVERSARIES

Sometimes memories of those anniversary years between the milestone anniversaries have a way of becoming lost.

◆

If you want to remember what you did on every anniversary — whether you spent a quiet evening at home together, had a romantic candlelight dinner for two or went on an exotic cruise — you can summarize the major details on the Wedding Anniversary pages. The following pages will serve to clarify and enhance the beautiful events of your marriage.

◆

WEDDING ANNIVERSARIES

YEARS MARRIED	HOW CELEBRATED *(location, activities, others present)*	GIFTS
19___ ☐		
19___ ☐		
19___ ☐		
19___ ☐		
19___ ☐		

ADDITIONAL REMARKS

YEAR   COMMENTS

19____

19____

19____

19____

19____

CHILDREN'S MILESTONES

If you are already using baby books, children's scrapbooks and photo albums available for recording your children's activities, the following pages of brief summaries will complement those records very well.

◆

Every page provides space for recording major accomplishments for each child. Activities and achievements in school, Scouts, 4-H, sports, music, dance, camp or hobbies can be highlighted on a single page.

◆

What fun it will be for you and the children to look at these yearly summary pages and read about their milestones years from now!

◆

CHILDREN'S MILESTONES

19____

CHILD	AGE	ACTIVITIES, ACHIEVEMENTS, EVENTS

CHILDREN'S MILESTONES

19____

CHILD	AGE	ACTIVITIES, ACHIEVEMENTS, EVENTS
_____	____	_____

CHILDREN'S MILESTONES

19____

CHILD	AGE	ACTIVITIES, ACHIEVEMENTS, EVENTS

CHILDREN'S MILESTONES

19____

CHILD   AGE   ACTIVITIES, ACHIEVEMENTS, EVENTS

CHILDREN'S MILESTONES

19____

CHILD	AGE	ACTIVITIES, ACHIEVEMENTS, EVENTS
_____	____	_____
_____	____	_____
_____	____	_____
_____	____	_____
_____	____	_____

ADDITIONAL REMARKS

YEAR   COMMENTS

19____

19____

19____

19____

19____

TRIPS & VACATIONS

Getting away from it all often means traveling to different and
interesting places where you can relax, see new sights
and meet new people.

◆

Was this the year the family took the Colorado raft trip? Did
you take part in a volunteer service trip helping researchers band
pelicans or dig for artifacts in Mexico? Often the things you do
and the people you meet are more memorable than the
actual site of the vacation.

◆

While traveling miles from home, did you meet some "new"
people who turned out to be neighbors on your street or
from your old home town?

◆

Be sure to write down the name of that favorite, romantic bistro
or out-of-the-way village you visited so that you may refer them
to friends or return yourself. Your vacation notes and specific
references can help you, in years to come, relive those pleasant
and stimulating experiences.

◆

TRIPS & VACATIONS

DATES   PLACES VISITED   OCCASION

19____

19____

19____

19____

19____

TRIPS & VACATIONS

FAMILY/FRIENDS

HIGHLIGHTS

ADDITIONAL REMARKS

YEAR COMMENTS

19____

19____

19____

19____

19____

GUESTS & VISITORS

If you have moved away from family and friends, you may have had the joy of having those special people visit your new home from time to time over the years.

◆

On the following page you can record who visited you and when they came. Whether you gave the "grand tour" of the major attractions in your city, sat up all night catching up on news about old acquaintances, or just provided comfortable accommodations for friends traveling through town, you will enjoy reading a brief description of these visits years from now.

◆

GUESTS & VISITORS

DATES   GUEST/VISITOR(S)   ACTIVITIES

19____

19____

19____

19____

19____

ADDITIONAL REMARKS

YEAR COMMENTS

19____

19____

19____

19____

19____

PARTIES HOSTED

Giving a party is a special event, whether it is an intimate dinner party or a full-house New Year's Eve celebration.

◆

If you enjoy giving parties you now have a place to keep a summary of the details. If there was a particular theme to your party, a special reason for celebrating, or an exceptional menu or recipe you can note this information for easy reference.

◆

There is also room for recording what you wore, the names of guests and any reflections you had after the party. The information you record will be fun to look back on and come in handy when you are planning future parties. If the party was large and requires more space for recording names of guests or other comments, use the Additional Remarks page following this section.

◆

PARTIES HOSTED

	DATES	ACTIVITIES *(attire, themes, event)*	MENU PLANNED
19___	_____	_____	_____

	DATES	ACTIVITIES *(attire, themes, event)*	MENU PLANNED
19___	_____	_____	_____

PARTIES HOSTED

GUESTS

REFLECTIONS

GUESTS

REFLECTIONS

PARTIES HOSTED

	DATES	ACTIVITIES *(attire, themes, event)*	MENU PLANNED
19____	_____	_____	_____

	DATES	ACTIVITIES *(attire, themes, event)*	MENU PLANNED
19____	_____	_____	_____

PARTIES HOSTED

GUESTS

REFLECTIONS

GUESTS

REFLECTIONS

PARTIES HOSTED

DATES   ACTIVITIES *(attire, themes, event)*   MENU PLANNED

19_____

PARTIES HOSTED

GUESTS

REFLECTIONS

ADDITIONAL REMARKS

YEAR COMMENTS

19____

19____

19____

19____

19____

ADDITIONAL EVENTS & RECORDS

All the other unique events, accomplishments, changes, and set-backs that occur in each year can be recorded on the following pages.

◆

A general list of ideas for activities you might want to include in this section under "Other" might include: winning a special prize or award, breaking a long-held record, getting your picture in the paper, meeting a famed personality, being elected as an officer in an organization or to a political position, completing a special project, or inheriting a treasured item.

◆

Use these pages to accommodate your personal interests. If you feel a particular event is more appropriate in a different section or in the Special Celebrations section of this book, move it to the place that best fits your needs.

◆

This book was designed for you and your family memories. Enjoy it.

◆

ADDITIONAL EVENTS & RECORDS

19____

BIRTHS:

WEDDINGS:

REUNIONS:

DEATHS:

MEDICAL RECORDS:

HOME IMPROVEMENTS:

ADDITIONAL EVENTS & RECORDS

MAJOR
PURCHASES: _____
_____
_____
_____

INVESTMENTS: _____
_____
_____
_____

EDUCATION: _____
_____
_____
_____

JOB CHANGES: _____
_____
_____
_____

WEATHER: _____
_____
_____
_____

OTHER: _____
_____
_____
_____

ADDITIONAL EVENTS & RECORDS

19_____

BIRTHS:

WEDDINGS:

REUNIONS:

DEATHS:

MEDICAL RECORDS:

HOME IMPROVEMENTS:

ADDITIONAL EVENTS & RECORDS

MAJOR
PURCHASES: _____
_____
_____
_____

INVESTMENTS: _____
_____
_____
_____

EDUCATION: _____
_____
_____
_____

JOB CHANGES: _____
_____
_____
_____

WEATHER: _____
_____
_____
_____

OTHER: _____
_____
_____
_____

ADDITIONAL EVENTS & RECORDS

19_____

BIRTHS:

WEDDINGS:

REUNIONS:

DEATHS:

MEDICAL RECORDS:

HOME IMPROVEMENTS:

ADDITIONAL EVENTS & RECORDS

MAJOR
PURCHASES: _____

_____

_____

_____

INVESTMENTS: _____

_____

_____

_____

EDUCATION: _____

_____

_____

_____

JOB CHANGES: _____

_____

_____

_____

WEATHER: _____

_____

_____

_____

OTHER: _____

_____

_____

_____

ADDITIONAL EVENTS & RECORDS

19_____

BIRTHS: _____
_____
_____

WEDDINGS: _____
_____
_____

REUNIONS: _____
_____
_____

DEATHS: _____
_____
_____

MEDICAL RECORDS: _____
_____
_____

HOME IMPROVEMENTS: _____
_____
_____
_____

ADDITIONAL EVENTS & RECORDS

MAJOR
PURCHASES: _____
_____
_____
_____

INVESTMENTS: _____
_____
_____
_____

EDUCATION: _____
_____
_____
_____

JOB CHANGES: _____
_____
_____
_____

WEATHER: _____
_____
_____
_____

OTHER: _____
_____
_____
_____

ADDITIONAL EVENTS & RECORDS

19_____

BIRTHS:

WEDDINGS:

REUNIONS:

DEATHS:

MEDICAL RECORDS:

HOME IMPROVEMENTS:

ADDITIONAL EVENTS & RECORDS

MAJOR
PURCHASES: _____
_____
_____
_____

INVESTMENTS: _____
_____
_____
_____

EDUCATION: _____
_____
_____
_____

JOB CHANGES: _____
_____
_____
_____

WEATHER: _____
_____
_____
_____

OTHER: _____
_____
_____
_____

ADDITIONAL REMARKS

YEAR COMMENTS

19____

19____

19____

19____

19____

MISCELLANEOUS

Books from LAWRENCE & COMPANY PUBLISHERS

THE FAMILY CHRONICLE by Judy Lawrence

Whether you are single, married, have a family or now retired, you will probably agree that in today's fast-paced world, the busy years just seem to pass by in a blur.

THE FAMILY CHRONICLE is an efficient way to keep track of highlights of those years. The book is designed to help you easily record the essence of the last five years worth of memories, information, and achievements.

THE FAMILY CHRONICLE is not only handy for you, but also makes a wonderful and practical birthday, wedding or anniversary gift for others.

$12.95

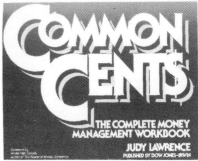

COMMON CENT$,
The Complete Money Management Workbook
by Judy Lawrence

COMMON CENT$, The Complete Money Management Workbook is a practical & useful day-to-day guide to help anyone gain control over their finances. Filled with 84 pages of money-saving management tips, monthly & yearly budget worksheets, and expense records. COMMON CENT$ makes an excellent & invaluable gift for yourself, a friend, or a relative.

$10.95

"In the last two years we went from $16,000 worth of debt to $2,000. We also saved over $5,300 and started a $3,500 retirement account. We never could have done it without your book!"

                         Albuquerque, New Mexico

"I can't tell you how much I enjoy using your publication. It gives me an opportunity to make specific decisions about where my paycheck ought to go for my personal well-being. Thank you again. You have a customer for life."

                            Ed Freeman, Baltimore MD

"COMMON CENT$ is brilliantly designed to be your first vital step down the road to financial independence. It provides you with a superbly organized workbook that enables you to account for each cent of your income."

                      Venita VanCaspel
                      Author of the best seller
                      THE POWER OF MONEY DYNAMICS

ORDER FORM

Name_____

Address_____

City_____ State_____ Zip_____

Phone_____

SEND CHECK OR MONEY ORDER TO: Lawrence & Co. Publishers
    P.O. Box 13167 • Albuquerque, New Mexico 87192
       or call 1-800-624-5893

Please send the following:

____THE FAMILY CHRONICLE $12.95.. _____

____COMMON CENTS $10.95.......... _____

            Subtotal _____

Add $1.50 Shipping & Handling

for 1 book, $.25 for each additional book_____

(N.M. Residents add 5.25% Sales Tax)_____

            TOTAL_____